Acts Of Paul And Thecla

William Wake

Kessinger Publishing's Rare Reprints

Thousands of Scarce and Hard-to-Find Books
on These and other Subjects!

- Americana
- Ancient Mysteries
- Animals
- Anthropology
- Architecture
- Arts
- Astrology
- Bibliographies
- Biographies & Memoirs
- Body, Mind & Spirit
- Business & Investing
- Children & Young Adult
- Collectibles
- Comparative Religions
- Crafts & Hobbies
- Earth Sciences
- Education
- Ephemera
- Fiction
- Folklore
- Geography
- Health & Diet
- History
- Hobbies & Leisure
- Humor
- Illustrated Books
- Language & Culture
- Law
- Life Sciences
- Literature
- Medicine & Pharmacy
- Metaphysical
- Music
- Mystery & Crime
- Mythology
- Natural History
- Outdoor & Nature
- Philosophy
- Poetry
- Political Science
- Science
- Psychiatry & Psychology
- Reference
- Religion & Spiritualism
- Rhetoric
- Sacred Books
- Science Fiction
- Science & Technology
- Self-Help
- Social Sciences
- Symbolism
- Theatre & Drama
- Theology
- Travel & Explorations
- War & Military
- Women
- Yoga
- *Plus Much More!*

We kindly invite you to view our catalog list at:
http://www.kessinger.net

2 I am thereby assured that I sow the most strong seed in a fertile soil, not any thing material, which is subject to corruption, but the durable word of God, which shall increase and bring forth fruit to eternity.

3 That which by your wisdom you have attained to, shall abide without decay for ever.

4 Believe that you ought to avoid the superstitions of Jews and Gentiles.

5 The things which you have in some measure arrived to, prudently make known to the emperor, his family, and to faithful friends;

6 And though your sentiments will seem disagreeable, and not be comprehended by them, seeing most of them will not regard your discourses, yet the Word of God once infused into them, will at length make them become new men, aspiring towards God.

7 Farewell, Seneca, who art most dear to us. Dated on the calends of August, in the consulship of Leo and Savinus.

The ACTS of PAUL and THECLA.

[Tertullian says that this piece was forged by a Presbyter of Asia, who being convicted, "confessed that he did it out of respect to Paul," and Pope Gelasius, in his Decree against Apocryphal books, inserted it among them. Notwithstanding this, a large part of the History was credited and looked upon as genuine among the primitive Christians. Cyprian, Eusebius, Epiphanius, Austin, Gregory Nazianzen, Chrysostom, and Severus Sulpitius, who all lived within the fourth century, mention Thecla, or refer to her history. Basil of Seleucia wrote her acts, sufferings, and victories, in verse; and Euagrius Scholasticus, an ecclesiastical historian, about 590, relates that "after the Emperor Zeno had abdicated his empire, and Basilik had taken possession of it, he had a vision of the holy and excellent martyr Thecla, who promised him the restoration of his empire; for which, when it was brought about, he erected and dedicated a most noble and sumptuous temple to this famous martyr Thecla, at Seleucia, a city of Isauria, and bestowed upon it very noble endowments, which (says the author) are preserved even till this day." Hist. Eccl. lib. 3. cap. 8.—Cardinal Baronius, Locrinus, Archbishop

Wake. and others; and also the learned Grabe, who edited the Septuagint, and revived the Acts of Paul and Thecla; consider them as having been written in the Apostolic age; as containing nothing superstitious, or disagreeing from the opinions and belief of those times; and, in short, as a genuine and authentic History. Again it is said, that this is not the original book of the early Christians; but however that may be, it is published from the Greek MS. in the Bodleian Library at Oxford, which Dr. Mills copied and transmitted to Dr. Grabe.]

The Martyrdom of the holy and glorious first Martyr and Apostle Thecla.

CHAP. I.

Demas and Hermogenes become Paul's companions. Paul visits Onesiphorus. Invited by Demas and Hermogenes. Preaches to the household of Onesiphorus. His sermon.

WHEN Paul went up to Iconium, after his flight from Antioch, Demas and Hermogenes became his companions, who were then full of hypocrisy.

2 But Paul looking only at the goodness of God, did them no harm, but loved them greatly.

3 Accordingly he endeavoured to make agreeable to them, all the oracles and doctrines of Christ, and the design of the Gospel of God's well-beloved Son, instructing them in the knowledge of Christ, as it was revealed to him.

4 And a certain man named Onesiphorus, hearing that Paul was come to Iconium, went out speedily to meet him, together with his wife Lectra, and his sons Simmia and Zeno, to invite him to their house.

5 For Titus had given them a description of Paul's personage, they as yet not knowing him in person, but only being acquainted with his character.

6 They went into the king's highway to Lystra, and stood there waiting for him, comparing all who passed by, with that description which Titus had given them.

7 At length they saw a man coming (namely, Paul), of a low stature, bald (or shaved) on the head, crooked thighs, handsome legs, hollow-eyed; had a crooked nose; full of grace; for sometimes he appeared as a man. sometimes he had the countenance of an angel. And Paul saw Onesiphorus, and was glad.

8 And Onesiphorus said: Hail, thou servant of the blessed God. Paul replied, The grace of God be with thee and thy family.

9 But Demas and Hermogenes were moved with envy, and, under a shew of religion, Demas said, And are not we also servants of the blessed God? Why didst thou not salute us?

10 Onesiphorus replied, Because I have not perceived in you the fruits of righteousness; nevertheless, if ye are of that sort, ye shall be welcome to my house also.

11 Then Paul went into the house of Onesiphorus, and there was great joy among the family on that account; and they employed themselves in prayer, breaking of bread, and hearing Paul preach the word of God concerning temperance and the resurrection, in the following manner:

12 Blessed are the pure in heart; for they shall see God.

13 Blessed are they who keep their flesh undefiled (or pure); for they shall be the temples of God.

14 Blessed are the temperate (or chaste); for God will reveal himself to them.

15 Blessed are they who abandon their secular enjoyments; for they shall be accepted of God.

16 Blessed are they who have wives, as though they had them not; for they shall be made angels of God.

17 Blessed are they who tremble at the word of God; for they shall be comforted.

18 Blessed are they who keep their baptism pure: for they shall find peace with the Father, Son, and Holy Ghost.

19 Blessed are they who pursue the wisdom (or doctrine) of Jesus Christ; for they shall be called the sons of the Most High.

20 Blessed are they who observe the instructions of Jesus Christ; for they shall dwell in eternal light.

21 Blessed are they, who for the love of Christ abandon the glories of the world; for they shall judge angels. and be placed at the right hand of Christ, and shall not suffer the bitterness of the last judgment.

22 Blessed are the bodies and souls of virgins: for they are acceptable to God, and shall not lose the reward of their virginity; for the word of their (heavenly) Father shall prove effectual to their salvation in the day of his Son, and they shall enjoy rest for evermore.

CHAP. II.

Thecla listens anxiously to Paul's preaching. Thamyris, her admirer, concerts with Theoclia her mother to dissuade her in vain. Demas and Hermogenes vilify Paul to Thamyris.

WHILE Paul was preaching this sermon in the

church which was in the house of Onesiphorus, a certain virgin named Thecla (whose mother's name was Theoclia, and who was betrothed to a man named Thamyris) sat at a certain window in her house,

2 From whence, by the advantage of a window in the house where Paul was, she both night and day heard Paul's sermons concerning God, concerning charity, concerning faith in Christ, and concerning prayer;

3 Nor would she depart from the window, till with exceeding joy she was subdued to the doctrines of faith.

4 At length, when she saw many women and virgins going in to Paul, she earnestly desired that she might be thought worthy to appear in his presence, and hear the word of Christ; for she had not yet seen Paul's person, but only heard his sermons, and that alone.

5 But when she would not be prevailed upon to depart from the window, her mother sent to Thamyris, who came with the greatest pleasure, as hoping now to marry her. Accordingly he said to Theoclia, Where is my Thecla?

6 Theoclia replied, Thamyris, I have something very strange to tell you; for Thecla, for the space of three days, will not move from the window, not so much as to eat or drink, but is so intent in hearing the artful and delusive discourses of a certain foreigner, that I perfectly admire, Thamyris, that a young woman, of her known modesty, will suffer herself to be so prevailed upon.

7 For that man has disturbed the whole city of Iconium, and even your Thecla, among others. All the women and young men flock to him to receive his doctrine; who, besides all the rest, tells them, that there is but one God, who alone is to be worshipped, and that we ought to live in chastity.

8 Notwithstanding this, my daughter Thecla, like a spider's web fastened to the window, is captivated by the discourses of Paul, and attends upon them with prodigious eagerness, and vast delight; and thus by attending on what he says the young woman is seduced. Now then do you go and speak to her, for she is betrothed to you.

9 Accordingly Thamyris went, and having saluted her, and taking care not to surprise her, he said, Thecla, my spouse, why sittest thou in this melancholy posture? What strange impressions

are made upon thee? Turn to Thamyris, and blush.

10 Her mother also spake to her after the same manner, and said, Child, why dost thou sit so melancholy, and, like one astonished, makest no reply?

11 Then they wept exceedingly; Thamyris, that he had lost his spouse; Theoclia, that she had lost her daughter; and the maids, that they had lost their mistress; and there was an universal mourning in the family.

12 But all these things made no impression upon Thecla, so as to incline her so much as to turn to them, and take notice of them; for she still regarded the discourses of Paul.

13 Then Thamyris ran forth into the street, to observe who they were that went in to Paul, and came out from him; and he saw two men engaged in a very warm dispute, and said to them;

14 Sirs, what business have you here; and who is that man within, belonging to you, who deludes the minds of men, both young men and virgins, persuading them, that they ought not to marry, but continue as they are?

15 I promise to give you a considerable sum, if ye will give me a just account of him; for I am the chief person of this city.

16 Demas and Hermogenes replied, We cannot so exactly tell who he is; but this we know, that he deprives young men of their (intended) wives, and virgins of their (intended) husbands, by teaching, There can be no future resurrection, unless ye continue in chastity, and do not defile your flesh.

CHAP. III.

They betray Paul. Thamyris arrests him with officers.

THEN said Thamyris, Come along with me to my house. and refresh yourselves. So they went to a very splendid entertainment, where there was wine in abundance, and very rich provision.

2 They were brought to a table richly spread, and made to drink plentifully by Thamyris, on account of the love he had for Thecla. and his desire to marry her.

3 Then Thamyris said, I desire ye would inform me what the doctrines of this Paul are, that I may understand them; for I am under no small concern about Thecla, seeing she so delights in that stranger's discourses, that I am in danger of losing my intended wife.

4 Then Demas and Hermogenes answered both together, and said, Let him be brought before the governor Castellius, as one who endeavours to persuade the people into the new religion of the Christians, and he, according to the order of Cæsar, will put him to death, by which means you will obtain your wife;

5 While we at the same time will teach her, that the resurrection which he speaks of, is already come, and consists in our having children; and that we then arose again, when we came to the knowledge of God.

6 Thamyris having this account from them, was filled with hot resentment;

7 And rising early in the morning, he went to the house of Onesiphorus, attended by the magistrates, the jailer, and a great multitude of people with staves, and said to Paul;

8 Thou hast perverted the city of Iconium, and, among the rest, Thecla, who is betrothed to me, so that now she will not marry me. Thou shalt therefore go with us to the governor Castellius.

9 And all the multitude cried out, Away with this impostor (magician), for he has perverted the minds of our wives, and all the people hearken to him.

CHAP. IV.

Paul accused before the governor by Thamyris. Defends himself. Is committed to prison, and visited by Thecla.

THEN Thamyris standing before the governor's judgment seat, spake with a loud voice in the following manner.

2 O governor, I know not whence this man cometh; but he is one who teaches that matrimony is unlawful. Command him therefore to declare before you for what reasons he publishes such doctrines.

3 While he was saying thus Demas and Hermogenes (whispered to Thamyris, and) said; Say that he is a Christian, and he will presently be put to death.

4 But the governor was more deliberate, and calling to Paul, he said, Who art thou? What dost thou teach? They seem to lay gross crimes to thy charge.

5 Paul then spake with a loud voice, saying, As I am now called to give an account, O governor, of my doctrines, I desire your audience.

6 That God, who is a God of vengeance, and who stands in need of nothing but the salvation of his creatures, has sent me to reclaim them from their wickedness and corruptions, from all (sinful)

pleasures, and from death;
and to persuade them to sin
no more.

7 On this account, God
sent his Son Jesus Christ,
whom I preach, and in whom
I instruct men to place their
hopes, as that person who
only had such compassion on
the deluded world, that it
might not, O governor, be
condemned, but have faith,
the fear of God, the knowledge of religion, and the
love of truth.

8 So that if I only teach
those things which I have
received by revelation from
God, where is my crime?

9 When the governor
heard this, he ordered Paul
to be bound, and to be put in
prison, till he should be more
at leisure to hear him more
fully.

10 But, in the night,
Thecla taking off her ear-
rings, gave them to the turn-
key of the prison, who then
opened the doors to her, and
let her in:

11 And when she made a
present of a silver looking-
glass, to the jailer, was
allowed to go into the room
where Paul was; then she
sat down at his feet, and
heard from him the great
things of God.

12 And as she perceived
Paul not to be afraid of
suffering, but that by divine
assistance he behaved himself with courage, her faith
so far increased, that she
kissed his chains.

CHAP. V.

*Thecla sought and found by her
relations. Brought with Paul
before the governor. Ordered to
be burnt, and Paul to be whipt.
Thecla miraculously saved.*

AT length Thecla was
missed, and sought for
by the family and by Tha-
myris in every street, as
though she had been lost;
till one of the porter's fellow-
servants told them, that she
had gone out in the night-
time.

2 Then they examined the
porter, and he told them,
that she had gone to the
prison to the strange man.

3 They went therefore
according to his direction,
and there found her; and
when they came out, they
got a mob together, and went
and told the governor all
that happened.

4 Upon which he ordered
Paul to be brought before his
judgment-seat.

5 Thecla in the mean time
lay wallowing on the ground
in the prison, in that same
place where Paul had sat to
teach her; upon which the
governor also ordered her to
be brought before his judgment-seat; which summons
she received with joy, and
went.

6 When Paul was brought thither, the mob with more vehemence cried out, He is a magician, let him die.

7 Nevertheless, the governor attended with pleasure upon Paul's discourses of the holy works of Christ; and, after a council called, he summoned Thecla, and said to her, Why do you not, according to the law of the Iconians, marry Thamyris?

8 She stood still, with her eyes fixed upon Paul; and finding she made no reply, Theoclia her mother cried out, saying, Let the unjust creature be burnt; let her be burnt in the midst of the theatre, for refusing Thamyris, that all women may learn from her to avoid such practices.

9 Then the governor was exceedingly concerned, and ordered Paul to be whipt out of the city, and Thecla to be burnt.

10 So the governor arose, and went immediately into the theatre; and all the people went forth to see the dismal sight.

11 But Thecla, just as a lamb in the wilderness looks every way to see his shepherd, looked around for Paul;

12 And as she was looking upon the multitude, she saw the Lord Jesus in the likeness of Paul, and said to her-self, Paul is come to see me in my distressed circumstances. And she fixed her eyes upon him; but he instantly ascended up to heaven, while she looked on him.

13 Then the young men and women brought wood and straw for the burning of Thecla; who, being brought naked to the stake, extorted tears from the governor, with surprise beholding the greatness of her beauty.

14 And when they had placed the wood in order, the people commanded her to go upon it; which she did, first making the sign of the cross.

15 Then the people set fire to the pile; though the flame was exceeding large, it did not touch her; for God took compassion on her, and caused a great eruption from the earth beneath, and a cloud from above to pour down great quantities of rain and hail.

16 Insomuch that by the rupture of the earth, very many were in great danger, and some were killed, the fire was extinguished, and Thecla preserved.

CHAP. VI.

Paul with Onesiphorus in a cave. Thecla discovers Paul; proffers to follow him; he exhorts her not for fear of fornication.

IN the mean time Paul, together with Onesiphorus, his wife and children, was keeping a fast in a certain cave, which was in the road from Iconium to Daphne.

2 And when they had fasted for several days, the children said to Paul, Father, we are hungry, and have not wherewithal to buy bread: for Onesiphorus had left all his substance, to follow Paul with his family.

3 Then Paul, taking off his coat, said to the boy, Go, child, and buy bread, and bring it hither.

4 But while the boy was buying the bread, he saw his neighbour Thecla, and was surprised, and said to her Thecla, where are you going?

5 She replied, I am in pursuit of Paul, having been delivered from the flames.

6 The boy then said, I will bring you to him, for he is under great concern on your account, and has been in prayer and fasting these six days.

7 When Thecla came to the cave, she found Paul upon his knees praying and saying, O holy Father, O Lord Jesus Christ, grant that the fire may not touch Thecla; but be her helper, for she is thy servant.

8 Thecla then standing behind him, cried out in the following words: O sovereign Lord, Creator of

heaven and earth, the Father of thy beloved and holy Son, I praise thee that thou hast preserved me from the fire, to see Paul again.

9 Paul then arose, and when he saw her, said, O God, who searchest the heart, Father of my Lord Jesus Christ, I praise thee that thou hast answered my prayer.

10 And there prevailed among them in the cave an entire affection to each other; Paul, Onesiphorus, and all that were with them being filled with joy.

11 They had five loaves, some herbs, and water, and they solaced each other in reflections upon the holy works of Christ.

12 Then said Thecla to Paul, If you be pleased with it, I will follow you whithersoever you go.

13 He replied to her, Persons are now much given to fornication, and you being handsome, I am afraid lest you should meet with greater temptation than the former, and should not withstand, but be overcome by it.

14 Thecla replied, Grant me only the seal of Christ, and no temptation shall affect me.

15 Paul answered, Thecla, Wait with patience, and you shall receive the gift of Christ.

9

CHAP. VII.

Paul and Thecla go to Antioch. Alexander a magistrate falls in love with Thecla, kisses her by force: she resists him: is carried before the governor, and condemned to be thrown to wild beasts.

THEN Paul sent back One-siphorus and his family to their own home, and taking Thecla along with him, went for Antioch;

2 And as soon as they came into the city, a certain Syrian, named Alexander, a magistrate in the city, who had done many considerable services for the city during his magistracy, saw Thecla, and fell in love with her, and endeavoured by many rich presents to engage Paul in his interest.

3 But Paul told him, I know not the woman of whom you speak, nor does she belong to me.

4 But he being a person of great power in Antioch, seized her in the street and kissed her; which Thecla would not bear, but looking about for Paul, cried out in a distressed loud tone, Force me not, who am a stranger; force me not, who am a servant of God; I am one of the principal persons of Iconium, and was obliged to leave that city, because I would not be married to Thamyris.

5 Then she laid hold on Alexander, tore his coat, and took his crown off his head, and made him appear ridiculous before all the people.

6 But Alexander, partly as he loved her, and partly being ashamed of what had been done, led her to the governor, and upon her confession of what she had done,[1] he condemned her to be thrown among the beasts.

CHAP. VIII.

Thecla entertained by Trifina; brought out to the wild beasts: a she-lion licks her feet. Trifina upon a vision of her deceased daughter, adopts Thecla, who is taken to the amphitheatre again.

WHICH when the people saw, they said: The judgments passed in this city are unjust. But Thecla desired the favour of the governor, that her chastity might not be attacked, but preserved till she should be cast to the beasts.

2 The governor then inquired, Who would entertain her; upon which a certain very rich widow, named Trifina, whose daughter was lately dead, desired that she might have the keeping of her; and she began to treat her in her house as her own daughter.

3 At length a day came,

---

[1] There being somewhat wanting here in the old Greek MS. it is supplied out of the old Latin version, which is in the Bodleian Library, Cod. Dig. 89, rather than out of Simeon Metaphrastes, a writer of the eleventh century.

when the beasts were to be brought forth to be seen; and Thecla was brought to the amphitheatre, and put into a den, in which was an exceeding fierce she-lion, in the presence of a multitude of spectators.

4 Trifina, without any surprise, accompanied Thecla, and the she-lion licked the feet of Thecla. The title written which denotes her crime, was, Sacrilege. Then the women cried out, O God, the judgments of this city are unrighteous.

5 After the beasts had been shewn, Trifina took Thecla home with her, and they went to bed; and behold, the daughter of Trifina, who was dead, appeared to her mother, and said; Mother, let the young woman, Thecla, be reputed by you as your daughter in my stead; and desire her that she would pray for me, that I may be translated to a state of happiness.

6 Upon which Trifina, with a mournful air, said, My daughter Falconilla has appeared to me, and ordered me to receive you in her room; wherefore I desire, Thecla, that you would pray for my daughter, that she may be translated into a state of happiness, and to life eternal.

7 When Thecla heard this, she immediately prayed to the Lord, and said: O Lord God of heaven and earth, Jesus Christ, thou Son of the Most High, grant that her daughter Falconilla may live for ever. Trifina hearing this, groaned again, and said: O unrighteous judgments! O unreasonable wickedness! that such a creature should (again) be cast to the beasts!

8 On the morrow, at break of day, Alexander came to Trifina's house, and said: The governor and the people are waiting; bring the criminal forth.

9 But Trifina ran in so violently upon him, that he was affrighted, and ran away. Trifina was one of the royal family; and she thus expressed her sorrow and said: Alas! I have trouble in my house on two accounts, and there is no one who will relieve me, either under the loss of my daughter, or my being unable to save Thecla. But now, O Lord God, be thou the helper of Thecla thy servant.

10 While she was thus engaged, the governor sent one of his own officers to bring Thecla. Trifina took her by the hand, and, going with her, said: I went with Falconilla to her grave, and now must go with Thecla to the beasts.

11 When Thecla heard this, she weeping prayed, and said: O Lord God, whom I have made my confidence and refuge, reward Trifina for her compassion to me, and preserving my chastity.

12 Upon this there was a great noise in the amphitheatre; the beasts roared, and the people cried out, Bring in the criminal.

13 But the women cried out, and said: Let the whole city suffer for such crimes; and order all of us, O governor, to the same punishment. O unjust judgment! O cruel sight!

14 Others said, Let the whole city be destroyed for this vile action. Kill us all, O governor. O cruel sight! O unrighteous judgment.

CHAP. IX.

Thecla thrown naked to the wild beasts; they all refuse to attack her: throws herself into a pit of water. Other wild beasts refuse her. Tied to wild bulls. Miraculously saved. Released. Entertained by Trifina.

THEN Thecla was taken out of the hand of Trifina, stripped naked, had a girdle put on, and thrown into the place appointed for fighting with the beasts: and the lions and the bears were let loose upon her.

2 But a she-lion, which was of all the most fierce, ran to Thecla, and fell down at her feet. Upon which the multitude of women shouted aloud.

3 Then a she-bear ran fiercely towards her; but the she-lion met the bear, and tore it in pieces.

4 Again, a he-lion, who had been wont to devour men, and which belonged to Alexander, ran towards her; but the she-lion encountered the he-lion, and they killed each other.

5 Then the women were under a greater concern, because the she-lion, which had helped Thecla, was dead.

6 Afterwards they brought out many other wild beasts; but Thecla stood with her hands stretched towards heaven, and prayed; and when she had done praying, she turned about, and saw a pit of water, and said, Now it is a proper time for me to be baptised.

7 Accordingly she threw herself into the water, and said, In thy name, O my Lord Jesus Christ, I am this last day baptised. The women and the people seeing this, cried out, and said, Do not throw yourself into the water. And the governor himself cried out, to think that the fish (sea-calves) were like to devour so much beauty.

8 Notwithstanding all this, Thecla threw herself into the water in the name of our Lord Jesus Christ.

9 But the fish (sea-calves), when they saw the lightning and fire, were killed, and swam dead upon the surface of the water, and a cloud of fire surrounded Thecla; so that as the beasts could not come near her, so the people could not see her nakedness.

10 Yet they turned other wild beasts upon her; upon which they made a very mournful outcry; and some of them scattered spikenard, others cassia, others amomus (a sort of spikenard, or the herb Jerusalem, or ladies-rose) others ointment; so that the quantity of ointment was large, in proportion to the number of people; and upon this all the beasts lay as though they had been fast asleep, and did not touch Thecla.

11 Whereupon Alexander said to the governor, I have some very terrible bulls; let us bind her to them. To which the governor, with concern, replied, You may do what you think fit.

12 Then they put a cord round Thecla's waist, which bound also her feet, and with it tied her to the bulls, to whose privy-parts they applied red-hot irons, that so they being the more tor-mented, might more violently drag Thecla about, till they had killed her.

13 The bulls accordingly tore about, making a most hideous noise; but the flame which was about Thecla, burnt off the cords which were fastened to the members of the bulls, and she stood in the middle of the stage, as unconcerned as if she had not been bound.

14 But in the mean time Trifina, who sat upon one of the benches, fainted away and died; upon which the whole city was under a very great concern.

15 And Alexander himself was afraid, and desired the governor, saying: I intreat you, take compassion on me and the city, and release this woman, who has fought with the beasts; lest both you and I, and the whole city, be destroyed:

16 For if Cæsar should have any account of what has passed now, he will certainly immediately destroy the city, because Trifina, a person of royal extract, and a relation of his, is dead upon her seat.

17 Upon this the governor called Thecla from among the beasts to him, and said to her, Who art thou? and what are thy circumstances, that not one of the beasts will touch thee?

18 Thecla replied to him: I am a servant of the living God; and as to my state, I am a believer on Jesus Christ his Son, in whom God is well pleased; and for that reason none of the beasts could touch me.

19 He alone is the way to eternal salvation, and the foundation of eternal life. He is a refuge to those who are in distress; a support to the afflicted, hope and defence to those who are hopeless; and, in a word, all those who do not believe on him, shall not live, but suffer eternal death.

20 When the governor heard these things, he ordered her clothes to be brought, and said to her, Put on your clothes.

21 Thecla replied: May that God who clothed me when I was naked among the beasts, in the day of judgment clothe your soul with the robe of salvation! Then she took her clothes, and put them on; and the governor immediately published an order in these words: I release to you Thecla, the servant of God.

22 Upon which the women all cried out together with a loud voice, and with one accord gave praise unto God, and said: There is but one God, who is the God of Thecla; the one God, who hath delivered Thecla.

23 So loud were their voices, that the whole city seemed to be shaken; and Trifina herself heard the glad tidings, and arose again, and ran with the multitude to meet Thecla; and embracing her, said: Now I believe there shall be a resurrection of the dead; now I am persuaded that my daughter is alive. Come therefore home with me, my daughter Thecla, and I will make over all that I have to you.

24 So Thecla went with Trifina, and was entertained there a few days, teaching her the word of the Lord, whereby many young women were converted; and there was great joy in the family of Trifina.

25 But Thecla longed to see Paul, and inquired and sent every where to find him; and when at length she was informed that he was at Myra in Lycia, she took with her many young men and women; and putting on a girdle, and dressing herself in the habit of a man, she went to him to Myra in Lycia, and there found Paul preaching the word of God; and she stood by him among the throng.

CHAP. X.

*Thecla visits Paul, visits Onesiph-
orus, visits her mother, who*

repulses her. Is tempted by the devil. Works miracles.

BUT it was no small surprise to Paul, when he saw her and the people with her; for he imagined some fresh trial was coming upon them;

2 Which when Thecla perceived, she said to him: I have been baptised, O Paul; for he who assists you in preaching, has assisted me to baptise.

3 Then Paul took her, and led her to the house of Hermes; and Thecla related to Paul all that had befallen her in Antioch, insomuch that Paul exceedingly wondered; and all who heard were confirmed in the faith, and prayed for Trifina's happiness.

4 Then Thecla arose, and said to Paul. I am going to Iconium. Paul replied to her: Go, and teach the word of the Lord.

5 But Trifina had sent large sums of money to Paul, and also clothing by the hands of Thecla, for the relief of the poor.

6 So Thecla went to Iconium. And when she came to the house of Onesiphorus. she fell down upon the floor where Paul had sat and preached, and, mixing tears with her prayers, she praised and glorified God in the following words:

7 O Lord, the God of this house, in which I was first enlightened by thee; O Jesus, Son of the living God, who wast my helper before the governor, my helper in the fire, and my helper among the beasts; thou alone art God for ever and ever, Amen.

8 Thecla now (on her return) found Thamyris dead, but her mother living. So calling her mother, she said to her: Theoclia, my mother, is it possible for you to be brought to a belief, that there is but one Lord God, who dwells in the heavens? If you desire great riches, God will give them to you by me; if you want your daughter again, here I am.

9 These and many other things she represented to her mother, (endeavouring) to persuade her (to her own opinion). But her mother Theoclia gave no credit to the things which were said by the martyr Thecla.

10 So that Thecla perceiving she discoursed to no purpose, signing her whole body with the sign (of the cross), left the house, and went to Daphne; and when she came there, she went to the cave, where she had found Paul with Onesiphorus, and fell down upon the ground, and wept before God.

11 When she departed thence, she went to Seleucia,

and enlightened many in the knowledge of Christ.

12 And a bright cloud conducted her in the journey.

13 And after she had arrived at Seleucia, she went to a place out of the city, about the distance of a furlong, being afraid of the inhabitants, because they were worshippers of idols.

14 And she was led (by the cloud) into a mountain called Calamon, or Rodeon. There she abode many years, and underwent a great many grievous temptations of the devil, which she bore in a becoming manner, by the assistance which she had from Christ.

15 At length certain gentlewomen hearing of the virgin Thecla, went to her, and were instructed by her in the oracles of God, and many of them abandoned this world, and led a monastic life with her.

16 Hereby a good report was spread every where of Thecla, and she wrought several (miraculous) cures, so that all the city and adjacent countries brought their sick to that mountain, and before they came as far as the door of the cave, they were instantly cured of whatsoever distemper they had.

17 The unclean spirits were cast out, making a noise; all received their sick made whole, and glorified God, who had bestowed such power on the virgin Thecla;

18 Insomuch that the physicians of Seleucia were now of no more account, and lost all the profit of their trade, because no one regarded them; upon which they were filled with envy, and began to contrive what methods to take with this servant of Christ.

CHAP. XI.

Is attempted to be ravished, escapes by a rock opening, and closing miraculously.

THE devil then suggested bad advice to their minds; and being on a certain day met together to consult, they reasoned amongst each other thus: The virgin is a priestess of the great goddess Diana, and whatsoever she requests of her, is granted, because she is a virgin, and so is beloved by all the gods:

2 Now then let us procure some rakish fellows, and after we have made them sufficiently drunk, and given them a good sum of money, let us order them to go and debauch this virgin, promising them, if they do it, a larger reward.

3 (For they thus concluded among themselves, that if they be able to debauch her, the gods will no more regard

her, nor Diana cure the sick for her.)

4 They proceeded according to this resolution, and the fellows went to the mountain, and as fierce as lions to the cave, knocking at the door.

5 The holy martyr Thecla, relying upon the God in whom she believed, opened the door, although she was before apprised of their design, and said to them, Young men, what is your business?

6 They replied, Is there any one within, whose name is Thecla? She answered, What would you have with her? They said, We have a mind to lie with her.

7 The blessed Thecla answered: Though I am a mean old woman, I am the servant of my Lord Jesus Christ; and though you have a vile design against me, ye shall not be able to accomplish it. They replied: It is impossible but we must be able to do with you what we have a mind.

8 And while they were saying this, they laid hold on her by main force, and would have ravished her. Then she with the (greatest) mildness said to them: Young men, have patience, and see the glory of the Lord.

9 And while they held her, she looked up to heaven, and said: O God most reverend, to whom none can be likened; who makest thyself glorious over thine enemies; who didst deliver me from the fire, and didst not give me up to Thamyris, didst not give me up to Alexander; who deliveredst me from the wild beasts; who didst preserve me in deep waters; who hast every where been my helper, and hast glorified thy name in me;

10 Now also deliver me from the hands of these wicked and unreasonable men, nor suffer them to debauch my chastity, which I have hitherto preserved for thy honour; for I love thee, and long for thee, and worship thee, O Father, Son, and Holy Ghost, for evermore. Amen.

11 Then came a voice from heaven, saying, Fear not, Thecla, my faithful servant, for I am with thee. Look, and see the place which is opened for thee: there thy eternal abode shall be; there thou shalt receive the (beatific) vision.

12 The blessed Thecla observing, saw the rock opened, to as large a degree as that a man might enter in; she did as she was commanded, bravely fled from the vile crew, and went into the rock, which instantly so closed, that there was not

any crack visible where it had opened.

13 The men stood perfectly astonished at so prodigious a miracle, and had no power to detain the servant of God; but only, catching hold of her veil, (or hood) they tore off a piece of it;

14 And even that was by the permission of God, for the confirmation of their faith, who should come to see this venerable place, and to convey blessings to those in succeeding ages, who should believe on our Lord Jesus Christ from a pure heart.

15 Thus suffered that first martyr and apostle of God, and virgin, Thecla; who came from Iconium at eighteen years of age; afterwards, partly in journeys and travels, and partly in a monastic life in the cave, she lived seventy-two years; so that she was ninety years old when the Lord translated her.

16 Thus ends her life.

17 The day which is kept sacred to her memory, is the twenty-fourth of September, to the glory of the Father, and the Son, and the Holy Ghost, now and for evermore. Amen.

The FIRST EPISTLE of CLEMENT to the CORINTHIANS.

[Clement was a disciple of Peter, and afterwards Bishop of Rome. Clemens Alexandrinus calls him an apostle, Jerome says he was an apostolical man, and Rufinus, that he was *almost* an apostle. Eusebius calls this the wonderful Epistle of St. Clement, and says that it was publicly read in the assemblies of the primitive church. It is included in one of the ancient collections of the Canon of Scripture. Its genuineness has been much questioned, particularly by Photius, patriarch of Constantinople in the ninth century, who objects, that Clement speaks of worlds beyond the ocean; that he has not written worthily of the divinity of Christ; and that, to prove the possibility of a future resurrection, he introduces the fabulous story of the phœnix's revival from its own ashes. To the latter objection, Archbishop Wake replies, that the generality of the ancient Fathers have made use of the same instance in proof of the same point; and asks, if St. Clement really believed that there was such a bird, and that it did

This is the end of this publication.

Any remaining blank pages are for our book binding
requirements and are blank on purpose.

To search thousands of interesting publications like this one,
please remember to visit our website at:

http://www.kessinger.net

CPSIA information can be obtained
at www.ICGtesting.com
Printed in the USA
BVHW060531020619
549916BV00008B/440/P